The
Mayo
Brothers

The Mayo Brothers

BY JANE GOODSELL

Illustrated by Louis S. Glanzman

Thomas Y. Crowell Company
New York

CROWELL BIOGRAPHIES

Edited by Susan Bartlett Weber

JANE ADDAMS *by Gail Faithfull Keller*
LEONARD BERNSTEIN *by Molly Cone*
MARTHA BERRY *by Mary Kay Phelan*
WILT CHAMBERLAIN *by Kenneth Rudeen*
CESAR CHAVEZ *by Ruth Franchere*
SAMUEL CLEMENS *by Charles Michael Daugherty*
CHARLES DREW *by Roland Bertol*
THE MAYO BROTHERS *by Jane Goodsell*
GORDON PARKS *by Midge Turk*
THE RINGLING BROTHERS *by Molly Cone*
JACKIE ROBINSON *by Kenneth Rudeen*
ELEANOR ROOSEVELT *by Jane Goodsell*
MARIA TALLCHIEF *by Tobi Tobias*
JIM THORPE *by Thomas Fall*
MALCOLM X *by Arnold Adoff*

MANUFACTURED IN THE UNITED STATES OF AMERICA

L.C. Card 70-139104   ISBN 0-690-52750-0   0-690-52751-9 (LB)

1 2 3 4 5 6 7 8 9 10

The
Mayo
Brothers

Will Mayo and his brother Charlie did most everything together. They played marbles and fished. They read stories and took turns churning cream into butter for their mother. Together they scrambled up the steep hills above the valley to hunt for Indian arrowheads. There were lots of arrowheads to be found around the little country town of Rochester, Minnesota, in 1873. Not so long ago Indians had roamed the hills and prairies with their bows and arrows.

The Mayo brothers did not look alike. Will, who was twelve years old, was tall and slim. He had blond hair and blue eyes. Charlie, who was eight, was squarely built. His eyes and hair were brown.

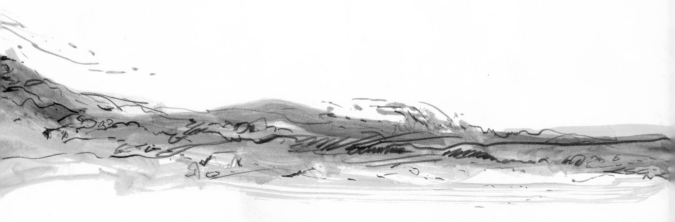

The boys were different in other ways, too. Will was strong and daring. He was a good rider, and he loved to gallop through town on his horse. But Will did not find it easy to make friends. He stayed a little apart from other people, and he had a quick temper.

Charlie was easygoing and had many friends. He sometimes got into mischief with them. But his friendly way with people often saved him from being punished.

The old janitor who rang the school bell liked Charlie and hated to see him get into trouble. The Mayos lived across from the school on Franklin Street. Charlie often ran home at recess for something to eat. He did not always get back to school before recess was over. If he was not at his desk by the time the bell stopped ringing, he was punished for being late. But the old janitor watched out for Charlie. He did not stop ringing the bell until he was sure that Charlie Mayo was safely in his seat.

Charlie was not much good at spelling, but he could do almost anything with his hands. If a stove did not work or a door squeaked, he could fix it. Will admired him for that, just as Charlie admired Will for his skill at riding.

The boys had many chores to do. They chopped wood and carried water from the well.

They helped their mother do the washing and weed the vegetable garden. Will and Charlie liked to be with their lively and cheerful mother. She talked to them about books she read. She explained how plants get their food from the soil and how they grow.

She taught them about stars and planets, too. She had her own telescope. It was in a tower on top of the Mayo house. Will and Charlie loved to look at the night sky through the telescope. It made the faraway stars seem very close.

5

Will and Charlie helped their father in his work, too. He was a doctor, and a very busy one. Dr. William Mayo saw no reason why his sons should not learn to roll bandages and scrub instruments.

He often took them with him when he went in his horse and buggy to visit sick people. The boys watched their father look down patients' throats and listen to their heartbeats. Later Dr. Mayo would explain how he knew what was wrong with the patients. He told the boys what he had done to make them better.

Dr. Mayo was a surgeon, too. He performed operations. Often Will and Charlie stood by their father's side to help him. There was no hospital in Rochester then. Surgery was done in people's homes. The boys learned to hand their father the instruments he needed. They helped to make plaster casts to set broken arms and legs.

Dr. Mayo often answered their questions by handing them a book to read. "Here," he said, "this book will help you understand how the blood flows through the body." Or he said, "Look at this drawing of the knee. Now you'll see what I'm talking about."

He showed Will and Charlie how to use a microscope. When they looked into it, they saw what a drop of blood or a chip of bone looks like. A microscope makes things appear many times larger than their real size.

Dr. Mayo taught his sons that a doctor should help sick people even if they have no money to pay him. Dr. Mayo did not like to send bills to poor people, although he needed money for his own family.

The Mayos were not poor. They lived in a nice house and they had a fine horse and buggy. But they were not rich either. Dr. Mayo had to borrow money to buy a new microscope. That seemed to him more important than new clothes and furniture. Will and Charlie wore their father's old suits. Their mother made the suits over to fit them.

When Will was old enough, he got a summer job in a drugstore. He swept floors and washed bottles. He spent his first month's pay to buy Charlie a new suit. It made Will feel proud to see his brother in his first store-bought suit.

Later Charlie worked in the same drugstore. He wanted to do what his older brother did.

When Will was nineteen years old, he went to the University of Michigan to study medicine. He was going to be a doctor. It had never entered his head that he might be anything else.

After three years Will finished his studies. He went home to Rochester as Dr. Will Mayo, to work in his father's office. Dr. William Mayo was glad to have his son to help him. Will was lucky, too, to work with his father. Dr. William Mayo was one of the best surgeons in that part of the country.

But it was not easy for Will at first. When sick people sent for Dr. Mayo, they did not mean young Dr. Will. Many times Will was sent back to tell his father to come instead. But Will's father had faith in his son. Often he said to Will, "You go right back and say you're just as good a doctor as I am. And tell them that I told you to say so."

Will had faith in himself, too. He knew exactly what he wanted to do with his life. One night a friend of his father's asked Will where he planned to go when he left Rochester. "You're an ambitious young man," the friend said. "Surely you don't plan to stay here in this little country town?"

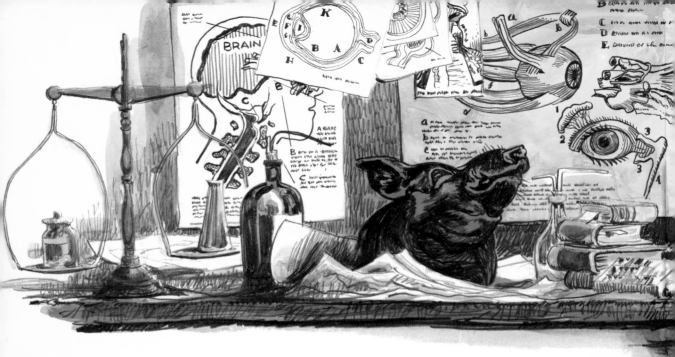

Will's answer was quick and sure. "I'm going to stay right here and become a great surgeon."

But Will knew that he still had much to learn. He began by studying diseases of the eye. Rochester needed a doctor to do eye surgery. Will read in medical books everything he could find about the eye. Then he practiced surgery on pigs and sheep that had been killed for butchering.

Finally he felt ready to operate on humans. He did three operations on people who were

DISCARDED

The Bright School
Chattanooga, Tennessee

blind. They were old and had no money to pay him. But Will did not care about that. The important thing was that two of the operations worked. The people could see again.

Will worked and studied hard. But sometimes he put his books aside for a party or a picnic. Often he asked Hattie Damon to go with him. She was a dark-haired girl who was rather shy. Will felt happy when he was with her.

Will and Hattie were married. Their first home was the house on Franklin Street where Will had lived as a boy. His parents had moved from there to a home in the country.

Then it was Charlie's turn to study medicine. He went to the Chicago Medical School. Like Will, he had always known that he wanted to be a doctor.

When Charlie finished school he returned to Rochester. Now there were three Mayo doctors working together in an office. It was a very modern office for that time. It had gaslights and running water.

By then Will and Hattie had a baby daughter named Carrie. Will was making enough money to move his family into a big new house. People trusted Will as a doctor now. He had many patients.

But Charlie was just Will's younger brother, fresh out of medical school. Now it was *his* turn to be sent back to the office to tell his

father to come instead. For a while Charlie grew a beard. He hoped that it would make him look older and more dignified.

But it was not Charlie's beard that won respect for him. It was his hands. They were as good at surgery as they were at fixing pumps and stoves. Soon it did not matter that Charlie looked young. People knew that he was a very good doctor.

Charlie did the first operation in the town's new hospital. The hospital was built because a terrible thing had happened to Rochester.

On a hot August day in 1883 a tornado hit the little town on the prairie. In just a few seconds buildings were ripped from the ground. Roofs broke loose and were whirled away in the howling wind. Houses shattered into bits and pieces. Thirty-five people were killed and hundreds were hurt.

In the hard rain that came after the storm, the job of rescue began. A large empty building was turned into a hospital. Dr. William Mayo was in charge of it. He sent Will and Charlie to the office to take care of the people who were brought there.

Everyone who was able helped those who were hurt or homeless. Women cooked food

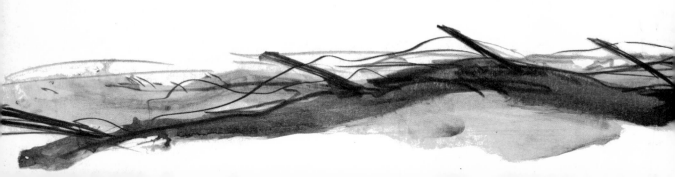

and made up beds. A group of nuns served as nurses. They were called the Sisters of Saint Francis. The nuns had not been trained for nursing. They were teachers. But they learned quickly what had to be done.

Other cities sent money to rebuild the town. But it was a long time before life was normal again in Rochester.

Yet this dreadful tragedy led to a wonderful idea. The Sisters of Saint Francis had saved some money. They wanted to use it to build a hospital in Rochester. They asked Dr. William Mayo to help them plan the building and run the hospital. At first he said no. The hospital would cost more money than the nuns could pay. "Besides," he said, "I'm too old."

"Your sons will carry on," the sisters told him. Dr. Mayo knew that this was true.

The nuns sewed and gave music lessons to make more money. They saved every penny they could. Four years after the tornado they had enough money to start the hospital. It was built in the country a mile from town. The sisters named it Saint Mary's Hospital.

The four-story brick building opened its doors to sick people in 1889. There was very little furniture because money had run out. The nuns' beds were moved into the rooms for patients. The sisters slept on mattresses on the floor. There was no running water. The nuns carried water upstairs in buckets from the basement. Charlie built the operating table himself. He also made some of the instruments used for surgery.

The nuns nursed patients long hours every day. They did the laundry and cleaning too. They walked a mile to town each day to buy food for the hospital. Often they had to rush to the Mayo office to say that a doctor was suddenly needed at Saint Mary's. The hospital had no telephone.

The Mayo brothers worked long and hard, too. Their father put them in charge of the hospital. He was now seventy years old, and he felt that it was time for his sons to take over. Will and Charlie were pleased that he trusted them. They were glad, too, that their father was now free to do other things.

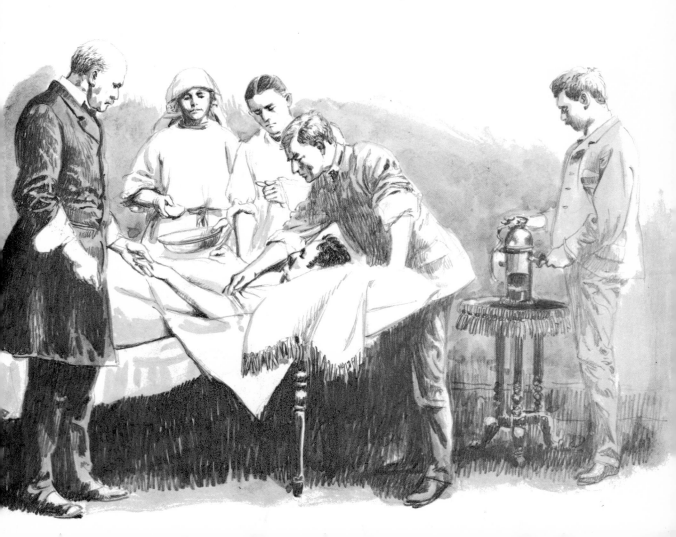

Old Dr. Mayo had many interests. He was active in city affairs and state politics. Also he was eager to travel. He went on working in the office, and he helped his sons at surgery. But they ran Saint Mary's. Will and Charlie took turns staying nights at the hospital when a doctor was needed there.

Saint Mary's had room for only forty-five patients when it opened. But it was not always filled, even though there were many sick people in Rochester. The reason for this seems strange to us today. At that time people were afraid of hospitals. They thought that anyone who went to a hospital was sure to die.

It is true that operations were then very dangerous. Many people became sick with infections after surgery. They got high fevers and often died. For a long time nobody knew how

DR. WILLIAM J. MAYO   DR. CHARLES H. MAYO

to keep this from happening. Then it was discovered that infections were caused by tiny germs, too small to be seen. If everything in an operating room was scrubbed with strong antiseptics, germs could not live to cause infections.

This was a very new idea at the time Saint Mary's opened. Many doctors did not believe in "antisepsis," as it was called. They thought it silly to worry about germs they could not

even see. But Will and Charlie insisted on absolute cleanliness when they operated. Because they were so careful, there were very few deaths in their hospital.

Soon people thought of Saint Mary's as a place to get well. Month by month more patients came. Before long the hospital earned enough money to buy furniture and pictures for the patients' rooms. A telephone system and an elevator were put in.

But it was not money that made Saint Mary's a famous hospital. It was knowledge. The Mayos never stopped learning and studying. They wanted to know everything they possibly could. They went all over the world to learn new ways to cure sickness.

There was much to learn during the hospital's early years. Many important discoveries in

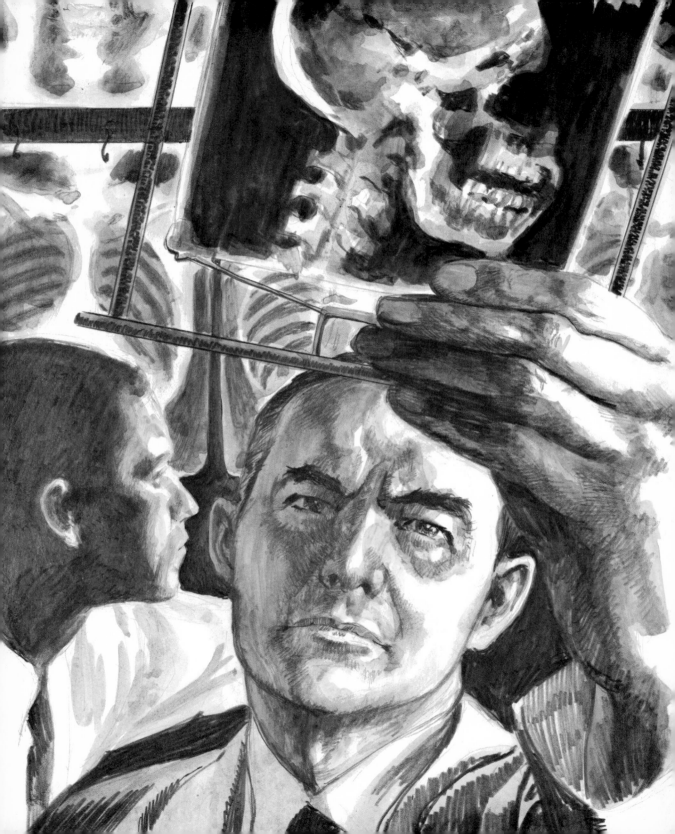

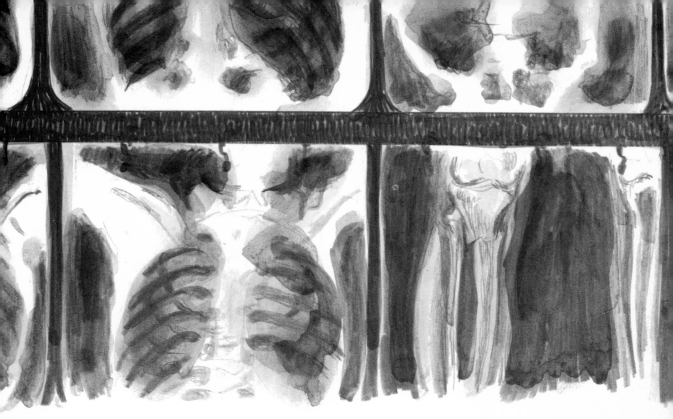

medicine were made. Doctors invented new ways to operate inside the body. Before antisepsis, they had not dared to do such operations. The risk of infection was too great.

They were helped by the X-ray, which was discovered by a German scientist. The X-ray camera took pictures of the inside of the body. Doctors learned many things from these pictures that they had not known before. The X-ray helped them find new ways to save lives.

Almost every day Will and Charlie read reports of new operations. Usually they were invented by doctors who worked in big hospitals in New York, Boston, Chicago, and Philadelphia. These doctors found ways to operate on the stomach, the chest, and the brain.

The Mayos wanted to visit other hospitals to learn how to do the new operations. So they began traveling. Dr. Will usually spent a month away in the fall. Dr. Charlie's turn came in the spring. In between, both took short trips. They made it a rule not to travel together. That way there was always a Dr. Mayo in Rochester to run Saint Mary's.

Will and Charlie were the only doctors for hundreds of miles around who knew how to do the new surgery. People traveled long distances to Rochester when they needed operations. The patients came because they knew people who had been cured by the Mayos. Many of them had been sick for years. They had been told by other doctors that there was no way to cure them. But they were made well again at Saint Mary's Hospital.

Doctors traveled to Rochester, too. Some came to watch the Mayos operate. Will was now one of the best stomach surgeons in the country. Charlie was an expert on bones and nerves and on the thyroid gland in the neck.

Other doctors came to scoff. They did not believe the stories they heard about the Mayos. How could two doctors perform almost four thousand operations in one year? Impossible!

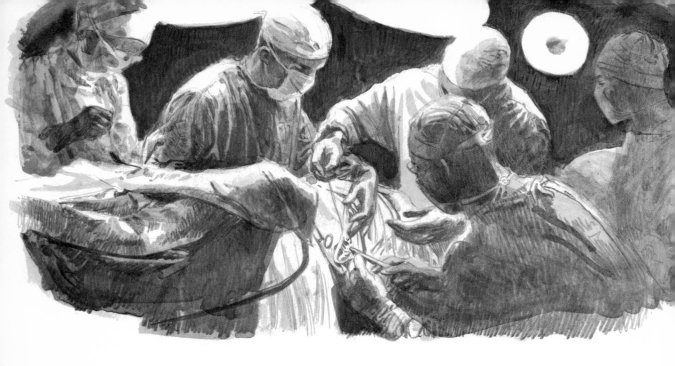

But the doctors found that the stories were true. One said in amazement that he had watched over one hundred operations in six days. Another doctor saw Will do ten operations in one morning.

Five years after Saint Mary's opened, its first addition was built. It had space for 135 more beds. Every few years after that, another wing was built. Little by little the hospital grew to be three blocks long.

Slowly and carefully the Mayos chose other doctors to work with them. They wanted men with special skills. One of their first partners was an expert on blood. He took charge of the laboratories where tests were made.

The Mayos often invited the other doctors and their families to go on summer picnics and winter sleigh rides. There were many parties at Will's and Charlie's houses.

Now Charlie was married, too. He had married pretty Edith Graham, the Mayos' office nurse. Their first home was next door to Will's and Hattie's.

Over the years, Charlie and Edith had a family of four girls and two boys. Will and Hattie had two daughters.

As men, the Mayo brothers were as different as they had been as boys. Will was formal and dignified, and always neatly dressed. People admired Will, but they were a little afraid of him. They did not laugh and joke with him as they did with Charlie. When patients felt sad, Charlie often sat beside their beds to cheer them up. He did not much care how he looked. His tie was usually crooked and his suit wrinkled.

The Mayo brothers were always best friends. They met each evening to talk about problems at the hospital. They did not always think alike. But decisions were not made until Will and Charlie agreed. "When Charlie says no," Will said, "it means no for me."

Each year brought more and more patients to the Mayo offices. In 1905, over ten thousand people were examined. By 1912, the number had risen to fifteen thousand. The Mayos then had dozens of doctors working with them. It was hard to find space in downtown Rochester for all the offices and laboratories that were needed. They were tucked in among the shops and restaurants that now crowded the town.

The Mayos decided that they must have a new building, large enough for everyone to work together under the same roof. They bought the property on Franklin Street where the old Mayo house stood. The house was torn down to make room for a big five-story building.

It opened in March 1914, and it was called the Mayo Clinic.

Patients came to this building to be examined —to find out what made them sick. This was done in a very special way at the Mayo Clinic.

Patients were not examined by one doctor but by many. They went from office to office. One doctor X-rayed their chests. Another tested their eyes. Still another looked down their throats or thumped their stomachs. They were examined from head to toes by experts. These doctors worked as a team to find out what was wrong and how best to make the patient well.

The Mayo Clinic practiced medicine in a new way. It was the first privately owned clinic in which doctors worked together as a group.

It became known as the greatest medical center in the world. Patients came to it by the hundreds of thousands. Some traveled from far corners of the earth to get there. A king from Arabia and a farmer from Kansas might pass each other in the halls. It was not surprising for a prince, a prime minister, and a famous

actress to show up on the same Monday morning.

Rochester became known all over the world as the home of the Mayo Clinic. It was no longer a little country town. It grew into a modern city with fine hotels, stores, parks, and museums.

Dr. William Mayo had died before the clinic opened. That made Will and Charlie very sad. They did not forget that their father had taken the first step that led to it. The Mayo Clinic really began with the little hospital built after the tornado.

Will's and Charlie's mother lived four years longer. Her sons knew that they owed much of their success to her, too. They often talked about her kindness and her sympathy for people. "We were born to the right parents," Will said.

The Mayo Clinic made a great deal of money. Will and Charlie became rich men. They had more than they needed for themselves and their families. The money came from sick people. The Mayos wanted to give it back in some way. They decided to do this by helping doctors learn more about sickness.

The Mayos gave more than two million dollars to the medical school at the University of Minnesota. The money was used to start a new program of classes. It was for doctors who wanted to go on studying. They learned new and better ways to cure sick people.

As Will and Charlie grew older, they made plans to give up their control of the clinic. They wanted to make sure that it would go on after they died. Gradually, they turned it over to a group of nine men to run. These men decided by vote what should be done.

Both Mayos operated on patients until 1928. Then Dr. Will was sixty-nine, and he announced that he would do no more surgery. "I want to quit while I'm still good," he said.

Dr. Charlie operated for the last time a year and a half later. On that day his son, Dr. Charles W. Mayo, did his first operation as a clinic surgeon.

Will and Charlie went on working as doctors. But now they were free to do other things. At last they could travel together, and they went on a trip to Europe.

Dr. Charlie spent much of his time at Mayo-wood, the country home he built a short distance from Rochester. He enjoyed farming and growing flowers. Dr. Will cruised rivers on his boat, the *North Star.* Both loved to have their families and friends around them.

It made them happy to watch the clinic continue to grow. They were glad that it could get along without them.

Both brothers died in 1939, within a few months of each other. But the Mayo Clinic lives on today, just as Will and Charlie planned.

ABOUT THE AUTHOR

Jane Goodsell, the author of THE MAYO BROTHERS, was born in Portland, Oregon, and has lived most of her life there. She has written books and magazine articles for both children and adults. She is married, and the mother of three daughters.

The father of one of Jane Goodsell's good friends worked with the Mayos in the early days of the clinic, and she has known many people who have been patients there.

"What interested me most in writing the book," Mrs. Goodsell says, "was the steadfast love, respect, and loyalty the brothers had for each other, and for their father, all their lives. They shared a dream, and they worked together to make it come true."

ABOUT THE ILLUSTRATOR

Louis Glanzman was raised in Virginia, but moved to New York when he was thirteen. By the age of sixteen he had started his creative work— writing and illustrating his own comic strip. Now a celebrated artist, he has illustrated a number of books and major-magazine covers. He is particularly famous for the widely known scene of Neil Armstrong setting foot on the moon, which was conceived in his mind and drawn for *Time* magazine two days *before* the actual event. In addition, some of his paintings are on display at the White House.

Mr. Glanzman lives on Long Island with his wife and four daughters.